1000 reasons for L♡VING YOU

Cluj-Napoca

2015

Copyright © Eduard Magiar

ISBN 978-973-0-18451-8

Facebook.com/1000.Reasons.Book

For me, this book is a declaration of
love and gratitude.

For you, it could be
anything.

If you need to choose what it is, do it, first, by listening
to your soul.
Whatever you decide to choose is right.

1. I love you because you are my little piece of Heaven.

2. I love you because you can transform my reality into magic dust.

3. I love you because you can dissolve the notion of distance.

4. I love you for the violence of your energy.

5. I love you because you flow through my veins faster than blood.

6. I love you because together we have more strength than the explosion of a Sun at its end.

7. I love you for the tears you offer me without asking for anything else in exchange.

8. I love you because you accept me as such even though I can be nothing more than a mirror for your soul.

9. I love you because you make the difference between happiness and sadness melt into one.

10. I love you because you are my beginning.

11. I love you because you can bring non-existent meanings into existence.

12. I love you because the essence of our love could never be described.

13. I love you because you showed me the only mistake of Buddha's philosophy, the elimination of desire.

14. I love you because of the one thousand different ways of kissing me without touching our lips.

15. I love you because you are my only religion.

16. I love you because every millimeter of your being can extract all the truths that I would ever need.

17. I love you because the Universe belongs to all, but you are my only Universe.

18. I love you because you suspend my thoughts in eternity.

19. I love you because you are what the alchemists were looking for.

20. I love you because you give me the confidence that I could finish to write a book in a day.

21. I love you because in every crack of your lips is a small paradise just waiting to be discovered.

22. I love you because your eyes can vaporize my soul.

23. I love you because your normality is my insanity.

24. I love you because I see all the beauty of the Universe lying in your eyes.

25. I love you because you are my flight into extraordinary.

26. I love you because every mystery you have is the starting point of hurricanes in my mind.

27. I love you because the sun becomes important only for the reason that you ARE.

28. I love you because every teardrop you shed is more precious to me than all the diamonds in the world.

29. I love you because I could get lost in your static vibrations.

30. I love you because you are the Angel of my inferno and the Demon of my dreams.

31. I love you because I NEED time off from you.

32. I love you for the ephemeral scent of your skin.

33. I love you because you make me fear I won't be able to find enough ways to tell you: "I love you".

34. I love you because no one could ever understand the bond we share.

35. I love you because every unspoken word of yours tells me more than a thousand other spoken.

36. I love you because what we create together help others find love.

37. I love you because no one else could be more vital than the air I breathe.

38. I love you because you are my fifth season.

39. I love you because your flame will always light my candle.

40. I love you because there's no need to tell me "I love you".

41. I love you because there's no need to tell you "I love you".

42. I love you because I can find you in any lyrics.

43. I love you because you are tattooed in my blood.

44. I love you because you needn't do anything for the simple reason that you do everything.

45. I love you because you decipher meanings that I don't want to be deciphered.

46. I love you because in you I find all nature's elements.

47. I love you because you have the sound of a shaman's drum in trance.

48. I love you for the vortex of your whisper.

49. I love you for your quality of being a cruel snake.

50. I love you because you make me push the right buttons only.

51. I love you because the end is just the beginning with you.

52. I love you because I can hear your silence in the form of the music of a fairy's flute.

53. I love you because you can turn my impatient moments into patience.

54. I love you because your bells can resonate stronger than all of the churches combined.

55. I love you because you can split reality into the most gentle way possibly desired.

56. I love you because you are the little that suffices me.

57. I love you because you are the chaos awaiting to erupt.

58. I love you because you are the only abundance that I would ever need.

59. I love you because this book doesn't need a table of contents.

60. I love you because you always choose to come back to me.

61. I love you because I can immerse into you.

62. I love you because you are "home" far from home.

63. I love you because you are esoteric even when you don't mean to.

64. I love you because you can build crystal towers without crystals.

65. I love you because you make the dark reveal its beautiful colors.

66. I love you because I want clowns at our wedding even though I don't plan one.

67. I love you because you can mold space and time.

68. I love you because everything will remain in our past.

69. I love you because you can explain a circle with the help of a square.

70. I love you for all the mysteries of the Universe, this being ours.

71. I love you because you are the oasis in my endless desert.

72. I love you because you are the exact combination between negative and positive.

73. I love you because no one will ever understand your language.

74. I love you because you can make half become whole.

75. I love you because you can align my thoughts in such a way as to become a divine symphony.

76. I love you because together we can weave the real and the unreal.

77. I love you because you forgive more than the Devil and punish more than God.

78. I love you because I will doubt no matter of how much you'll try to persuade me not to.

79. I love you because you are the nothing that the grow-ups fear.

80. I love you because you can bring laughter into every day's reality.

81. I love you because your name does NOT matter.

82. I love you for the transparency of your echo.

83. I love you because your time is not enough sometimes.

84. I love you because with you no morning will look the same.

85. I love you because music becomes real hallucination because of you.

86. I love you because it is the way to know the music of the universe.

87. I love you because you are my balance.

88. I love you because you make the time spin.

89. I love you because you are the dictionary I need to understand any extra-terrestrial language.

90. I love you because your goodwill only will give dandelions a chance in front of your breath.

91. I love you because you make the red be redder.

92. I love you because you are the ocean of sensuality I want to dive in.

93. I love you because I can fly on the surface of your lips.

94. I love you because you are my child with stars in your eyes.

95. I love you because you are that last piece of puzzle I don't want to put in its place.

96. I love you because you reveal what small expectations I have.

97. I love you because you use the whip to control in those precise moments of need.

98. I love you because we grow the most delicate flowers together.

99. I love you because you are the one who makes Shiva dance.

100. I love you because you are that mysterious element of the Indo-Iranian rituals.

101. I love you because I see myself when looking at you.

102. I love you because your pupils can create the most amazing multi-dimensional structures.

103. I love you because there is no logic left in the grammar of your non-physical presence.

104. I love you because we share a bond never to be untied.

105. I love you because all of my body particles stretch their limits depending on you.

106. I love you because you can't grow old if I don't let you.

107. I love you because I can find no reason not to.

108. I love you for your childish, guilty smile.

109. I love you for the perfection hidden in your shortest hair.

110. I love you for the ecstasy after the ecstasy you offer me without asking for anything in return.

111. I love you because you are my God.

112. I love you because you are the flag I fly under.

113. I love you because you are the beginning of every experience.

114. I love you because you create the flame for the stars to be born.

115. I love you because you can crush my bones in a sweet embrace.

116. I love you because the only ring I will ever give you will be that of the sun.

117. I love you because you are my cancer.

118. I love you because you turn metal into silk.

119. I love you because I understand my unearthly nature through you.

120. I love you because you bring the festival of Rio into every second of my existence.

121. I love you because my smile is always too exaggerated in your presence.

122. I love you because your heart beat sounds like a solo song of a guitar.

123. I love you because you are the only one who knows to tune my emotions.

124. I love you because you tailor the clothes of my insanity.

125. I love you because your truth is holy.

126. I love you because you can reverse all rhythms in a fraction of a second.

127. I love you for all the clichés that I will never get to whisper in your ears.

128. I love you because you can't become illegal.

129. I love you because you made me understand that sex is but the top of the iceberg.

130. I love you because we are tribal in the most modern way.

131. I love you because the rockets we launch go nowhere.

132. I love you because space is just the piano music you play.

133. I love you because you and only you can turn me on and off.

134. I love you because your fingertips can draw infinity of shades.

135. I love you because your skin makes everything matter.

136. I love you because you can make my blood freeze.

137. I love you because your fullness will never empty.

138. I love you because you make me be a wanderer.

139. I love you because you are my only real challenge.

140. I love you because I want nothing from you.

141. I love you because you are the tree of the forbidden apple.

142. I love you because you are the open window of every sunset.

143. I love you because you show me the privilege of becoming who I was.

144. I love you because you are my primary source.

145. I love you because you can erase the line between play and seriousness in seconds.

146. I love you because you are the ace in my royal flush.

147. I love you because you are the infinite of my end.

148. I love you because you are the picture that I will never paint.

149. I love you because you are my master and I your subject.

150. I love you because you are the yoga of my mind.

151. I love you because you can trace my lines with an invisible pencil.

152. I love you because life is just another feature you have.

153. I love you because you have the ferocity of a domestic cat.

154. I love you because you exhale undefined meanings.

155. I love you because you are the pirate of my treasures.

156. I love you because your being can crush all earthly religions.

157. I love you because you can turn grey into the most tinted of all colors.

158. I love you because you make my anxiety become safe.

159. I love you for those moments when you decide to lift me high up in the sky.

160. I love you because you are the reason for which they built the pyramids.

161. I love you because only I know how to worship you.

162. I love you because you are the mask of my anonymity.

163. I love you because you are the seed of my creativity.

164. I love you because I can reach the truth of other people through you.

165. I love you because you're the only sense I need.

166. I love you because you are the perfect representation of desire.

167. I love you because you are the veil that wipes my tears.

168. I love you because you make me feel there's no time though there is no rush.

169. I love you because you are the eraser of my imperfections.

170. I love you because I don't need a writing tool to write about my love for you.

171. I love you because I can't find a way to say no.

172. I love you because you are my bridge to eternity.

173. I love you because you are my clothes at any time.

174. I love you because I can easily replace you with dopamine.

175. I love you because you surprise me every time a try to get you.

176. I love you because you blow my intuition into pieces.

177. I love you for the nonconformism of your conformism.

178. I love you for the freedom of your ideas.

179. I love you because you do magic that only I can see.

180. I love you because you are my timeless clock.

181. I love you because your shadow is mine only.

182. I love you because you show me death with every sunrise.

183. I love you because you wait.

184. I love you because of the many poor souls to whom you bring disappointment.

185. I love you because our traffic lights will always show green.

186. I love you because your air is more pure than that of the highest mountain on earth.

187. I love you because you align my stars the way they should be aligned.

188. I love you because the only indestructible moment of freedom is you.

189. I love you because together we define harmony.

190. I love you because you are the arch for my arrows.

191. I love you because you bring light to my consciousness.

192. I love you because your slowest moves can make higher waves than any tsunami.

193. I love you because you offer me the best when I less expect it.

194. I love you because you are the spaceship of my imagination.

195. I love you because you are the double meaning of any song.

196. I love you because, when the Greek created the tragedy, you didn't exist.

197. I love you because you align my world to yours.

198. I love you because I couldn't tell you lies even if I wanted.

199. I love you because I can reach you in every spider web unwoven.

200. I love you because you can blend all the colors in just one.

201. I love you because you make me feel more sinless than after the first baptism.

202. I love you because you are the most royal amongst all wines.

203. I love you because you are my getaway to the first world.

204. I love you because you don't understand me even though you do.

205. I love you because you make me understand that I can't dwell into the past.

206. I love you because your forgiveness needs no reason.

207. I love you because you break my chains of fear.

208. I love you because you are my lighthouse through fog and haze.

209. I love you because you are the only child whose smile I'll ever want.

210. I love you because the rain of your clouds keeps me dry.

211. I love you because your message is more important than of Jesus'.

212. I love you because whenever you feel lonely I'll be there.

213. I love you because you are the only jewel of my crown.

214. I love you because you hold the essence of my beginning.

215. I love you because you are the only god I pray.

216. I love you because you are the reason I have been waiting for.

217. I love you because I won't lose as long as you're with me.
218. I love you because you make bipolarity sexual.

219. I love you because you are the only soldier I need to win all wars.

220. I love you because you fuse me with the Source.

221. I love you for the vanishing scent of your hair.

222. I love you because you make me shape mysteries.

223. I love you because angels have forgotten you.

224. I love you because of that audacity of being active in the vacuum of my atoms.

225. I love you because your skin's surface features of Venus.

226. I love you because you can be mad at me without I even realizing it.

227. I love you because your birth day is yours only.

228. I love you because you are the form my absurd.

229. I love you because you are the soul in my body.

230. I love you because you come before Alfa and after the Omega.

231. I love you because you made me understand that true poverty is the absence of your love.

232. I love you because you are my unconvicted criminal.

233. I love you because you may be more violent in revenge than in your love.

234. I love you because you can make me dance without the sound of music in the background.

235. I love you because you showed me that the most important of the apostles was Thomas.

236. I love you because you explained that Jesus was killed by people and reborn alone.

237. I love you because you are the Demon of my salvation.

238. I love you because through you I revived.

239. I love you because YOU ARE LOVE itself.

240. I love you because you're my capital sin that I will not cease to repeat.

241. I love you because the violence of your dictionary is more merciful than the Bible.

242. I love you because eros can save more souls than the righteousness of the Church.

243. I love you because you make humans regret they invented Satan.

244. I love you because you are the only ocean of truth that I could ever need.

245. I love you because you convince me that there's more ecstasy in Hell than in the Heaven of my sins.

246. I love you because I wear pleasure tattooed in my soul.

247. I love you because you're sensual beyond fears or lies.

248. I love you because our religion does not require a book of good practices.

249. I love you because there are no demands in the ecstatic moments you give me.

250. I love you because I have NO expectations!

251. I love you because I will offer me to carry your crucifix of your lies.

252. I love you because you showed me the Path of Love in just three words.

253. I love you because you show merciless grace.

254. I love you because you are the only dungeon I wish to be imprisoned.

255. I love you because you lent Judas silvers.

256. I love you because you lead an empire where kings and servants are all alike.

257. I love you because once you've whispered in my ear that authority is just another face of doubt.

258. I love you because the storm of our love sweeps away authority.

259. I love you because our home is their home.

260. I love you because in your love's massacre I find myself reborn.

261. I love you because every second with you is my resurrection.

262. I love you because the impulse of your lipstick leaves deeper traces than the word of the Lord.

263. I love you because you possess my mind first.

264. I love you because you don't have to forgive my sins.

265. I love you because you are the virtue that I don't need.

266. I love you because your double negations don't become affirmations.

267. I love you because you are my daily communion.

268. I love you because your lent is abundant.

269. I love you because you are my loving peace.

270. I love you because the song of your existence is all I need to write these words.

271. I love you because our Valentine's Day is every night.

272. I love you because your blood is mine.

273. I love you because your Holy Grail is a recyclable plastic cup.

274. I love you because you are my 8th Sin.

275. I love you because your sword can cut the thorns of roses, yet will never be used.

276. I love you because I can read the TRUTH written on your skin.

277. I love you because you make me accept my 7th sin as my first nature.

278. I love you because you are the risk I will not take.

279. I love you because I don't need megaphones buildings' corners to understand your message.

280. I love you because I don't have to confess myself to you, yet I willingly do.

281. I love you because the end of your pain is my only beginning.

282. I love you because "unique" is just an illogical word for you.

283. I love you because everybody else need further explanation to get you.

284. I love you because you inspired me these lines at the beginning of a new era.

285. I love you because you give me all your weaknesses with no desire to solve them.

286. I love you because you plunge my thoughts in the center of our universe!

287. I love you because your gravity is my creation.

288. I love you because I am your symbol.

289. I love you because you do not define the Trinity, you make it ONE.

290. I love you because you let me dive in the waters of your love.

291. I love you because you chose me with so much help you need to share.

292. I love you because I became food for thought through you.

293. I love you because I can only measure your value unless I bring all and nothing together.

294. I love you because I am nothing and you, EVERYTHING.

295. I love you because you reveal the limits of my foolishness.

296. I love you because together we have the creative force of three Gods combined.

297. I love you because no one and everybody will understand our reason to feel.

298. I love you because your time is not NOW, but ALWAYS.

299. I love you because the problem that we are can generate the final solution.

300. I love you because your direction is correct and simple.

301. I love you because your ladder can't be lowered.

302. I love you because I don't feel the urge of fitting you into an either round, borderless or badly numbered table.

303. I love you because I can begin any sentence I want with "I love you" and finish it with yourself.

304. I love you because the silence that I want to listen to is as divine as the noise made by the excessive number of decibels of your whisper.

305. I love you because it's you only who can guide me to the final point of oblivion.

306. I love you because my oblivion is your soul quantum mathematics.

307. I love you because you are the shaman vitality that lies in me.

308. I love you because you are my eternal return.

309. I love you because you are the tribute to my soul.

310. I love you for all the pointless arrows thrown that make sense because of you.

311. I love you because you are the water that satisfies my thirst with just one drop.

312. I love you because you'll feed me with the price of your life.

313. I love you because time decreases and expands when you dwell in my veins.

314. I love you because you make forget to number the reasons for which I love you.

315. I love you because the numbers lose their meaning in your presence.

316. I love you because you are the beam of light that passes through my window in the morning.

317. I love you because you remind me that we are the Nature.

318. I love you because you are my eternal life.

319. I love you because those who read the following lines will understand that it's all about them because of us.

320. I love you because the patience you give me you offer it without resentment to all of those who'll read this book further.

321. I love you because you make me regain my sanity.

322. I love you because thanks to you my writing is meditation.

323. I love you because you understand my silence.

324. I love you because you are my way of simplifying things.

325. I love you because you bring me the tranquility that I need.

326. I love you because thanks to you those who will continue to read this book are, and I will keep on repeating it, perfect beyond all limits of the word.

327. I love you because my love for you overflows on anyone who still reads these lines.

328. I love you because the only reason of my existence is you, and that is enough to summarize this book.

329. I love you because you made me understand how much I love myself, and for that I thank you every nano-second of my eternity.

330. I love you because I understand that the distance between us is but a mere illusion that we can simply blow away in seconds.

331. I love you because your sleep is the only reason for staying awake at night.

332. I love you because sometimes I need to invent new ways to say "I love you".

333. I love you because you are the slumbering beast inside my body.

334. I love you because you wake me up in the morning.

335. I love you because I feel it all for you.

336. I love you for those rare moments when I wish not to feel anything for you.

337. I love you because you are always by my side and inside.

338. I love you because I can feel you even when you don't want me to.

339. I love you because I make you cry sometimes.

340. I love you because I'll dry your tears with myself.

341. I love you because your smile in our first embrace will shine brighter than the sun itself.

342. I love you for every orgasm you'll give me without my ever doing anything.

343. I love you because out most real orgasms are mental.

344. I love you because you detail the concept of pleasure in the simplest ways.

345. I love you because making love to you is beyond any understanding.

346. I love you because you make my hands sweat by only thinking about you.

347. I love you because your name brings me on that fine line between reality and imagination.

348. I love you because you are the pause that I need and I need not.

349. I love you because you are my fairy dust.

350. I love you because you make me accept my ordinary self.

351. I love you because you make it impossible to hate you.

352. I love you because you name is unknown.

353. I love you because every time I believe to have disappointed you, you prove me wrong.

354. I love you because my schizophrenia is another side of your bipolarity.

355. I love you because I shall never give you up.

356. I love you because I can be whoever I want when we are together.

357. I love you because you never fail to anticipate my words.

358. I love you because I am your torch, and you gave me light.

359. I love you because you dress me up in colors.

360. I love you because our fingerprints are exactly the same.

361. I love you because our house have no walls.

362. I love you because you are my sport.

363. I love you because you are my wings to freedom.

364. I love you because you are the adventure that brings me a new sun every day.

365. I love you because you give me the benefit of the doubt.

366. I love you because you are the law court of my soul.

367. I love you because you taught me to write well.

368. I love you because I'm the center of your mandala.

369. I love you because I am drunk with the fragrance of your breasts.

370. I love you because you are the most pure mountain spring.

371. I love you because your nails create masterpieces on my skin.

372. I love you because you are the spice that gives me flavor.

373. I love you because you are a little bit more than my little.

374. I love you because you own my ultimate right to breathe.

375. I love you because you cut my heart open with no anesthetic.

376. I love you because the voices I hear are all yours.

377. I love you because you are my total eclipse of the evil.

378. I love you because with you I'm always on the edge.

379. I love you because you are my daily reading.

380. I love you because I wish I could do for you more than I can.

381. I love you because you chose to be my muse.

382. I love you because you are my favorite communication channel.

383. I love you because you are my earthquake, and I, your volcano.

384. I love you because you are the ink remaining my thoughts.

385. I love you because I need no ticket with you taking me to destination.

386. I love you for when we dance on the waves of pleasure.

387. I love you because your toy train is always full of passengers.

388. I love you because you write the script for the film of my life.

389. I love you because you are ready to be with me.

390. I love you because the arrows you throw are already in my heart.

391. I love you because you use me.

392. I love you for the illusion of your distrust.

393. I love you because you are the bank of my intangible values.

394. I love you for your toxic lips.

395. I love you for the genius of your insanity.

396. I love you because you are the artisan of my archaic revival.

397. I love you because only I can see the bruises of your soul.

398. I love you because you heal my memories.

399. I love you for the mountains and the oceans of your spine.

400. I love you because you offer me reasons to make you forget you have once been sane.

401. I love you because you are my magic evergreen forest.

402. I love you because, though you offer me nothing, I will not ever forget you.

403. I love you because you are my poisonous magic potion.

404. I love you because, had everything collapsed around us, I would have been the one to keep you standing.

405. I love you because you do not care.

406. I love you because the endless kiss of this very moment.

407. I love you because you are my judgment day.

408. I love you because we are in a fancy ball.

409. I love you because you hang on even when you feel the voice of your heart fading away.

410. I love you because you are the only cookbook without ingredients.

411. I love you because I am your guiding star when you need me.

412. I love you because you refuse the breath of my betrayal.

413. I love you because your roots feed from my soil.

414. I love you because you fill me by consuming me.

415. I love you because you alter me again and again.

416. I love you for your bitter taste.

417. I love you because I see you in every grain of sand in the hourglass.

418. I love you because you are my current practice.

419. I love you because we are Adam and Eve.

420. I love you because you set my body free.

421. I love you because I rewrite your destiny with a compass.

422. I love you because I laugh and you cry, I cry and you laugh.

423. I love you because you are my cosmic wound.

424. I love you because I can hear the whisper of the sea in the beating of your heart.

425. I love you because your memory will stay with me until the end.

426. I love you because you are the sky and the earth.

427. I love you because our calendar is a blank sheet of paper.

428. I love you because we are free to depend on each other.

429. I love you because I am not forced to think we can do better.

430. I love you because you are my celestial Ego.

431. I love you because you ask for things when I don't want to offer them.

432. I love you because you speak through me, and I through you.

433. I love you because you are stronger than I will ever be.

434. I love you for all that you could be, but are not.

435. I love you for all that you are and you could become.

436. I love you because you are the love letter in my mail box.

437. I love you because our essence of our love does not reside in details.

438. I love you because you make peace with my past.

439. I love you because you are the space between our beings.

440. I love you because you will be part of my past.

441. I love you because you asked me to forget you.

442. I love you because you hold on when I let go.

443. I love you because you strength my weak thoughts.

444. I love you because you leave every day only to come back.

445. I love you because you are the spirit of my heart.

446. I love you because you command the stars to guide us at night.

447. I love you because I need your mystery to survive.

448. I love you because I see your face in imaginary photos.

449. I love you because you are the exercise of my patience.

450. I love you because in your absence I'm the same.

451. I love you for the lines written between these pages.

452. I love you because you bring spring in winter.

453. I love you because shadows emerge from our ashes.

454. I love you because sometimes you think that my mistakes are yours.

455. I love you because you make me burn with no fire.

456. I love you because you are my new icon.

457. I love you because you stop and I begin.

458. I love you because I can stretch and touch your horizon.

459. I love you because you are the meteorite that shapes my moon.

460. I love you because you give me grace to touch the texture of your darkness.

461. I love you because you are the celebration of my tragic love.

462. I love you because I still love you.

463. I love you because I am the mirror of your future.

464. I love you because I beg for the crumbs of your existence.

465. I love you because you are the indistinct shape in the sunset.

466. I love you because you are the last drop of water in my glass.

467. I love you because you are my masterpiece yet unsigned.

468. I love you indecently.

469. I love you beyond love sometimes.

470. I will always love you as my book of wisdom.

471. I love you because you are the unwritten poem of my being.

472. I love you because I'm the poem of your blood.

473. I love you because you make any poem perfect.

474. I love you because I am on your destiny's agenda.

475. I love you in spite of not knowing who you are.

476. I love you because you put my love and patience to a test.

477. I love you because you have everything I'll ever need.

478. I love you because you are the proof of my faith.

479. I love you because you are the missing part of my soul I didn't know I lacked.

480. I love you because you broke my heart to pieces and put it back together.

481. I love you because you are my thirst and hunger.

482. I love you because our love is ageless.

483. I love you because your wish is my command.

484. I love you because I created you.

485. I love you because we are the actors in our own play.

486. I love you because you are the country I want to live in.

487. I love you because you remind me of the future.

488. I love you because you tempt me and then forgive my sins.

489. I love you because you are my innocent geisha.

490. I love you because you take my hand and fly to Neverland.

491. I love you because you bathe in the lakes on the moon.

492. I love you because I stand alone in the void of your absence.

493. I love you because you are my long polished pure sapphire.

494. I love you because your eyes are windows to a new world.

495. I love you because you always spell my name in the wrong way.

496. I love you for your flesh is vegan.

497. I love you because I'm reminded with every morning that you are my personal miracle.

498. I love you because you are the chaos that brings me to Order.

499. I love you because we transcend love.

500. I love you because you suffocate my ecstasy.

501. I love you because you are my guilty pleasure deeply carved in my brain.

502. I love you because you are my East in the West.

503. I love you because I am wrong when you prove me right.

504. I love you because your light does not make me blind.

505. I love you because you are my final chapter.

506. I love you because you are the bridge between myself and everybody else.

507. I love you because I was lost and you have found me.

508. I love you because you are the Light, the Truth, and the Way.

509. I love you because you are the dream in whose embrace I return every morning.

510. I love you because you are my only connection to the supreme truth.

511. I love you because I can find you in other people.

512. I love you because you've been here before, you lived and you loved.

513. I love you because you are my routine turned into extraordinary magic.

514. I love you because we've met too late, yet found each other too soon.

515. I love you because you talked to me about sorrow.

516. I love you because I can feel my eternity when in your embrace.

517. I love you because I'll be endlessly waiting for you.

518. I love you because by losing everything, you'll have me.

519. I love you because I am here with you there.

520. I love you because you are the only Sun whose heat I'll ever need.

521. I love you because you are brave enough to save the world.

522. I love you because I am your last option.

523. I love you for the healing power of our love.

524. I love you despite self-oblivion.

525. I love you because you bite my smile as if an apple.

526. I love you because you pause my flow.

527. I love you because you love me stubbornly.

528. I love you because you became a part of me.

529. I love you because you are the only angel I ever worshiped.

530. I love you because you are my universal echo.

531. I love you because you are my island in the sun.

532. I love you because my flame will not burn you if staying too close to me.

533. I love you for all the shapes choose to incarnate.

534. I love you because you express all expectations.

535. I love you because you always do what your heart tells.

536. I love you because your love is my infinite space to wander.

537. I love you because our time is timeless.

538. I love you for you are the flag that leads me towards my victories.

539. I love you because you've conquered me with no battle.

540. I love you because I'll be waiting for you on the other side of the map.

541. I love you because your love makes everything possible.

542. I love you because our steps are so differently similar.

543. I love you because I feel the thrill of your anticipation.

544. I love you because you are the precipice of my life.

545. I love you because you reflect the beauty of my soul.

546. I love you because I am aware I might lose you.

547. I love you because your existence is my abundance.

548. I love you because you understand the metaphor of our comparisons.

549. I love you because you are my irresistible desire.

550. I love you because you tune my harmonies to perfection.

551. I love you because we are above uncertainty.

552. I love you because you devour the remains of fear.

553. I love you because I am your voyage on far away seas.

554. I love you because you are the poem of my senses.

555. I love you because your love is my spiritual fire.

556. I love you because our friendship is inspired by beauty.

557. I love you because you give me reason to live.

558. I love you because you are my fantasy journey.

559. I love you because I know the geography of your body.

560. I love you because you are my tireless traveler.

561. I love you because you are the philosophy of my entire universe.

562. I love you because you make me listen what you do not say.

563. I love you because you wrap me in your love.

564. I love you because you are my hidden source of energy.

565. I love you because you make the impossible possible.

566. I love you because the power of our love knows no limits.

567. I love you because the curls of your hair are more dangerous than snakes.

568. I love you for you have a cat's nine lives.

569. I love you because you sing live while my song is just playback.

570. I love you because you kneel my desire.

571. I love you because 'you make me so happy that...'

572. I love you because you set the trend of my temper.

573. I love you because your beauty is priceless.

574. I love you for the storms you have inside.

575. I love you because your words are mine.

576. I love you because my mental dissolution is your deed only.

577. I love you because there's no rush in your gestures.

578. I love you because your motives are uncertain.

579. I love you because your uncertainty is certain.

580. I love you because I am the seed of your pleasure.

581. I love you because I am you and you are me.

582. I love you because you are my context.

583. I love you because I don't need a context to love you.

584. I love you because you are my reason to be proud.

585. I love you because I am your humble servant.

586. I love you because you praise me.

587. I love you because the curves of your body are more flexible than any line.

588. I love you because you are my inner monster.

589. I love you because you do not hide under my bed at night.

590. I love you because your love is the sleep of my consciousness.

591. I love you for you are my breath of fresh air.

592. I love you because you are my only family.

593. I love you because you let me fall so I can rise.

594. I love you because with nothing but one touch you mesmerize me entirely.

595. I love you because you are my bond to everlasting happiness.

596. I love you because your "yes" is pure.

597. I love you because your "yes" is divine.

598. I love you because your "yes" is wild.

599. I love you because your "yes" is profound.

600. I love you because your "yes" is eternal.

601. I love you because your "yes" is sexual.

602. I love you because your "yes" is mysterious.

603. I love you because my "yes" is you.

604. I love you because you are the queen of my private show.

605. I love you because I am your Inquisition.

606. I love you because you are the guillotine of my pain.

607. I love you because your eyes are daggers of your silence.

608. I love you because my kiss is your eternal damnation.

609. I love you because your touch is my short lived solace.

610. I love you because my death gives you life.

611. I love you because we can dance on our silent music.

612. I love you because the answer of your questions is me.

613. I love you because your lies are my truth.

614. I love you because you offer me freedom of choice by giving just one option.

615. I love you because your love is my fearless enemy.

616. I love you because you are the violence of my peace.

617. I love you because you are the victory of my wars.

618. I love you because I am the victim of your love.

619. I love you because I am restless without your love.

620. I love you because we always make plans together.

621. I love you because I don't have to smoke you to inhale you.

622. I love you because you are natural.

623. I love you because you are creative.

624. I love you because you are relaxing.

625. I love you because you are fearless.

626. I love you because you make me love.

627. I love you because you make me love more.

628. I love you because you cure me.

629. I love you because you are mystical.

630. I love you because you are peaceful.

631. I love you because you heal my pain.

632. I love you because you should be illegal.

633. I love you because you always reach my lost sense of humor.

634. I love you because all we have is NOW.

635. I love you because you always manage to make me smile.

636. I love you because I find you in every corner of my soul.

637. I love you for our voice together is stronger than a rock.

638. I love you because you are my abyss.

639. I love you because you are my duality.

640. I love you because I am your therapy.

641. I love you for the virtual reality you created around us.

642. I love you because your happiness is more important than my own.

643. I love you because you are the strength of my present.

644. I love you because I am the sanctuary of your soul.

645. I love you because you make me shout of my passion.

646. I love you because you are my longing for home.

647. I love you because you remind me the significance of the present.

648. I love you because you are my guru.

649. I love you because I dare be your fault.

650. I love you because your story does not need telling.

651. I love you because you are my most colorful rainbow.

652. I love you because you are my sacred totem.

653. I love you because your love is an art form.

654. I love you because you are my only intuition.

655. I love you because you are the future of my children.

656. I love you because you are my innocent fetish.

657. I love you because you are the past of my present.

658. I love you because you are my perfect pattern.

659. I love you because you are liquid geometry in pure state.

660. I love you because you are my surviving strategy.

661. I love you because you consume my time.

662. I love you because I am the sign you trust.

663. I love you because your fragrance is in minute details.

664. I love you because I'm your most human soul.

665. I love you because you wander through my thoughts as if you were home.

666. I love you more by staying away from you.

667. I love you because you are my magic carpet ready to fly with me into the immensity of the universe.

668. I love you because you are the magic mist wrapping my universe.

669. I love you because your scent reminds me of the child I was.

670. I live you because you are the potion that makes me drunk.

671. I love you because the sunrise has no colour.

672. I love you because without you the flowers in spring no longer bloom.

673. I love you because you're my favorite addiction.

674. I love you because stars smile at me every time I think about you.

675. I love you for your overwhelming sex appeal.

676. I love you because you are a dream.

677. I love you because you make me jealous beyond reason.

678. I love you because time struggles to change you.

679. I love you because you make me feel I could be forever young.

680. I love you because life with you is better than the most wonderful dream.

681. I love you because we could turn our love story into a film and win at the Oscars.

682. I love you because I don't need a pet since I have you.

683. I love you because you are my most generous backpack.

684. I love you for your endless patience while listening to my nonsense.

685. I love you because your eyes put a spell on me.

686. I love you because I don't need porn to masturbate since I've known you.

687. I love you because you and angels look alike.

688. I love you because you burst into tears after your orgasms.

689. I love you because sex with you is like a menage a trois.

690. I love you because you give me shivers with your touch.

691. I love you because white becomes colour in your presence.

692. I love you because you do the monkey dance.

693. I love you because you love water just as much as a little frog.

694. I love you because you're my favorite ringtone.

695. I love you because only manage you push all my buttons.

696. I love you because you make me want to be I better man.

697. I love you because sometimes you have no limits.

698. I love you because you make me seriously consider becoming a vegetarian.

699. I love you because I no longer have fantasies since I've met you.

700. I love you because life is a playground for you.

701. I love you because, just like a four-year-old, you don't like to lose.

702. I love you because my love for you goes beyond the margins of the universe.

703. I love you because put me in my place and for that I thank you.

704. I love you because I don't even remember how it would be not to.

705. I love you because you make me believe I'm the strongest in the world.

706. I love you because you've managed to drive me insane.

707. I love you because I have more than a thousand reasons to.

708. I love you because you taught me to listen to the grass grow.

709. I love you because you showed me how to fly without leaving your arms.

710. I love you because in you I found the other half of my soul.

711. I love you because you've filled me with so much happiness that I can share it with the whole world.

712. I love you for teaching me that an embrace can last for a lifetime.

713. I love you because your eyes have filled my whole universe with that beautiful look.

714. I love you for bringing your charm into my life.

715. I love you for being the center of my universe.

716. I love you for the sunshine in your eyes.

717. I love you because your smile speaks about human kindness to the world.

718. I love you because you turn the seconds into colours and give them meaning.

719. I love you for you're so noble to make me believe that it's ok to be myself no matter what.

720. I love you because, although I don't always rise to the height of your expectations, I am still a great winner in your eyes.

721. I love you because you show me the beauty of life and make me live it to its fullest.

722. I love you because you take me as I am, with my smooth and rougher edges.

723. I love you because each time you join me to pass the bound of hope.

724. I love you because you're my inspiration when I need it the most.

725. I love you because when you smile I feel I can be whoever I want.

726. I love you because you taught me the lesson of being kind with myself, trustworthy with the others and warm with such a wonderful creature as you.

727. I love you for I've learned to build spiritual bridges because of you.

728. I love you because you've taught me how to make my first joint.

729. I love you because no one else is so patient when I drink too much.

730. I love you because you offered your help to write this book.

731. I love you because you brought me to rehab twice.

732. I love you because you've showed me a new way to use stamps.

733. I love you for asking what else we could use the stamps for.

734. I love you because you make me weep a colorful rainbow.

735. I love you for bringing the teenager in me to light.

736. I love you because the sound of your voice is sweeter than any melody.

737. I love you because you heal my loveless sick soul.

738. I love you because you're the essence my being.

739. I love you because you've crushed my heart under the force of your love.

740. I love you because you know how to make kneel before you.

741. I love you for you are the most beautiful creature that have ever lived in my universe.

742. I love you because you brighten my day with just a smile.

743. I love you because you eat the fries on my plate even though you're not hungry.

744. I love you because you scent is sweeter than the most expensive fragrance.

745. I love you because your lips make me shiver when you don't let me kiss them.

746. I love your freckles in the summer.

747. I love you because I'm ashamed of loving the child that you still are.

748. I love you because you blush when I give you flowers.

749. I love you because you're not afraid to cry on my shoulder.

750. I love you because you are.

751. I love you because to confess you'd missed me while I was away.

752. I love you because your heart fits perfectly in the empty space that used to be my heart.

753. I love you for nobody else should love you but me.

754. I love you because you like the taste of my spells.

755. I love you because only you know what we did last summer.

756. I love you so you won't fade.

757. I love you because I'm not aware of what I'm doing.

758. I love you because even though I knew what I was doing, I could not stop.

759. I love you because my love could ground you.

760. I love you for everything you are and will be.

761. I love you for the evenings in tears and the mornings in laughter.

762. I love you for you shall never leave me.

763. I love you because I can't hate you.

764. I love you for all the sunny days and starry nights.

765. I love you for I feel you deep inside my soul.

766. I love you because you make me feel myself.

767. I love you because I fall asleep dreaming of you.

768. I love you because what I live when I'm with you has no comparison to any pill of ex.

769. I love you because you're the pleasure of my soul.

770. I love you because I am myself when I'm with you.

771. I love you because together we are the beginning with no end.

772. I love you because God gave me the grace of turning my life not into a tavern but into a temple because of you.

773. I love you because it doesn't matter what I have but WHO I have in my life.

774. I love you because when I met you the sun became brighter.

775. I love you because you made me successful with a fearless soul by my side.

776. I love you for the challenge of winning you heart every day.

777. I love you because, with you in my arms, space and time blend into a relative mass

778. I love you because you are the salt and pepper in my life.

779. I love you because, when I see you by my side, I just know that the most wonderful journey of my life is about to begin.

780. I love you because you give me the chance of always missing you.

781. I love you because you are the only one in whose abyss I can find myself.

782. I love you because, even though I am constantly under siege, it is you who win every time.

783. I love you because you are the only one who realizes that sometimes, most of the times, regardless of the position of my body, my soul is always on its knees.

784. I love you because you know to lie to me so remarkably well.

785. I love you because you give meaning to my existence.

786. I love you because by your side I can feel the caress of the most delicate of roses.

787. I love you because it is next to you I feel the greatness of the most beautiful feelings of all.

788. I love you because you unconditionally offered me you heart.

789. I love you because you prove the loyalty of your love to me with every moment.

790. I love you because you taught me that a smile can banish all the sadness of our hardships.

791. I love you for allowing me to be your shadow even if the sun doesn't shine.

792. I love you because love cannot be superlative; it either exists or not.

793. I love you because you have taught me to love September sunsets just as much as a summer's morning sunrise.

794. I love you because you believed in our telepathy.

795. I love you because you taught me that criticism is not always productive.

796. I love you for your lack of vanity.

797. I love you for your puppy eyes when I'm upset with you.

798. I love you because you always apologize when you're wrong.

799. I love you because you don't take personally everything I do.

800. I love you for your great unique sense of humor.

801. I love you because when you take your shirt off I can no longer focus on my laptop.

802. I love you because you still make me blush when you make compliments.

803. I love you because if we were on a deserted island the only thing I would miss would be my computer.

804. I love you because you trust me completely.

805. I love you because you bring me back when I go astray from the right path.

806. I love you because I'm convinced that we're soul mates.

807. I love you because you forgave me a thousand times before and you will always do.

808. I love you for you're so honest that you make me feel bad.

809. I love you for you're the only one who's shown endless indulgence to my weird hobbies.

810. I love you because you are my musical muse.

811. I love you because you made me give up smoking.

812. I love you because you're the strangest programming language I've ever met.

813. I love you because no one else would beep me on Skype.

814. I love you because if you didn't exist in my life, all the things in my house would be perfectly arranged at their place.

815. I love you because you made me climb the highest peaks of sexuality.

816. I love you because I love winter just because you love it, too.

817. I love you because you love me even when I've forgotten to love myself.

818. I love you for the incredible patience with which you let life to happen.

819. I love you for your contagious optimism.

820. I love you because you know how to harness life.

821. I love you because God created you for me and me only.

822. I love you because you are my religion, my daily bread and my guardian angel.

823. I love you because no matter how far you are from me, we've never been closer.

824. I love you because you are on my side defending me even when I don't deserve it.

825. I love you because you made my love my life instead of hating it as I used to do before knowing you.

826. I love you because you were my salvation from the bitter loneliness in which I thought I was doomed to live forever.

827. I love you because only you take me to climax and then bring me back into your arms.

828. I love you because you want many beautiful children with me.

829. I love you for all those hot teas you make whenever I catch a cold.

830. I love you for the surprises you make with or without a reason.

831. I love you because you are my mentor, my teacher, my role model.

832. I love you because I don't know how to love somebody else but you.

833. I love you because you are patient.

834. I love you because you've taught me to love myself for who I am.

835. I love you because you live in the present and speak about love.

836. I love you because of the thousand wonderful moments together.

837. I love you for the thousand wonderful moments that are yet to come.

838. I love you because you came into my life when I needed you the most.

839. I love you because to take me as I am, good or bad.

840. I love you for you revealed a different world from the one I used to know, more beautiful, more interesting, more kind.

841. I love you for you save my soul from dying every single day.

842. I love you because you're the only one who pokes me on Facebook.

843. I love you for all the life's lessons that you are willing to share with me.

844. I love you for seeing in me what the others have missed.

845. I love you for trusting me.

846. I love you for being by my side for better or worse.

847. I love you because there nobody else like you; there has never been and will never be.

848. I love you because you are my peace and quiet coming true.

849. I love you and thank you for shaping our life together.

850. I love you because you're my lucky star.

851. I love you because you're my soul's oxytocin.

852. I love you because you make me better.

853. I love you because you're continuously growing stock.

854. I love you because you make me feel like I am the richest person in the world when I'm with you.

855. I love you because you give me courage to climb the highest mountains.

856. I love you for you know compassion.

857. I love you because you make me chill in hot summers.

858. I love you for how you use to play with my curls.

859. I love you because you are in love with nature.

860. I love you for how you fool around and make me laugh.

861. I love you for being my best friend.

862. I love you because you awaken the beast in me.

863. I love you because you give me hope.

864. I love you because you don't fear mistake.

865. I love you because you search me with your eyes, your heart, your soul, with your whole being.

866. I love you because you know who you are.

867. I love you for the duplicity of your personality.

868. I love you because you're the shaman's dance in the universe fall.

869. I love you because you're the alluring coffee aroma in the morning.

870. I love you because you know to feast from the happiness of others.

871. I love you because you have a bigger heart than Santa Claus.

872. I love you because you make my rainy days shine.

873. I love you for you are the best person that ever stepped into my life.

874. I love you for taking the time to understand me even when I'm not worthy of your attention.

875. I love you because you are not afraid to love me.

876. I love you because you took me under your wing.

877. I love you for the adorable way you are with me.

878. I love you for all the special moments we've had together.

879. I love you for your soft silky touch.

880. I love you because you're the cutest person I know.

881. I love you because we'll be the most adorable two old people in love.

882. I love you because you hear what I have to say.

883. I love you because you can't get enough of my looking at you.

884. I love you because you confess your true feelings.

885. I love you because I want to get up in the mornings with the sound of your voice.

886. I love you because with you every day is summer.

887. I love you for the light in your eyes when you look at me.

888. I love you because you take my demons into your hands and make them fly as white doves in the sky.

889. I love you because you are the first and the last person I ever think about.

890. I love you because you never give up.

891. I love you because you've shown me that opposites attract.

892. I love you because not a day that goes by that you don't show your love for me.

893. I love you because I've forgotten all pain and sorrows since the day I met you.

894. I love you because you have the courage to confront me whenever I do silly things.

895. I love you because I can't imagine a picture without you in it.

896. I love you because sine we've met there's nothing I want to change in my life.

897. I love you because you know who I am whereas I don't really know myself.

898. I love you for showing me that fantasies can become real.

899. I love you for our long conversations without words.

900. I love you because you can watch a two hour movie with me although you don't like genre.

901. I love you because when I'm with you I completely forget about the rest of the world.

902. I love you because you let me warm my hands and feet with the heat of your body.

903. I love you because you are the one I want next to my coffee in the morning.

904. I love you because every time we kiss it's like the first time.

905. I love you because you have the proof that cats and dogs can live together.

906. I love you because every time I listen to blues I think of us.

907. I love you for showing me that of some things I never get enough.

908. I love you because it feels like childhood Christmases each time we spend the holidays together.

909. I love you because you always see he bright side of everything.

910. I love you because you banished "I can't" from the vocabulary.

911. I love you because every day away from you causes me excruciating pain.

912. I love you because spending Saturday nights with you on a sofa watching movies is better than going out.

913. I love you because you understand I need to feel free.

914. I love you because you tolerate the misplaced jokes I make sometimes.

915. I love you because you join me to KFC even though you're vegetarian.

916. I love you because you're willing to share with me even your last Haribo jelly.

917. I love you because of your most amazingly beautiful aura.

918. I love you because we share the same sadness whenever we come across some poor old man in the street.

919. I love you because you love summer just as much as I do.

920. I love you because I know that if you had enough money there wouldn't be poor people in this world.

921. I love you because you're the first person who's ever made me want children.

922. I love you because you pretend to like my cooking although I know it's not that great.

923. I love the way you show your love to me when we're in public.

924. I love the way we make peace after we fight.

925. I love you because you want to be with me and only me from the whole world.

926. I love you because your love is wild and rough.

927. I love you because you make me laugh when I don't even want to smile.

928. I love you for the way we finish each other's sentence.

929. I love you for the cuddling in each other's arms to watch the sun going down.

930. I love you for you let to live my life in freedom yet every day by your side.

931. I love you for the way you hold my hand.

932. I love you because you make me fall in love with you again and again.

933. I love you for you give me space when I need it.

934. I love you because you don't mind the marks I make on your body out of too much love.

935. I love you because I'm at my best when I'm with you.

936. I love you because you forgive all the little silly things I do.

937. I love you because you're funny when you drink a little too much.

938. I love you because you take me dancing even though you hate to dance.

939. I love you because you drain my vital energy only to give it back.

940. I love you because I can still see the child in you when you ask me to play together.

941. I love you because you admit your lust for me.

942. I love you because you turn the poker games into my favor although I don't really know to play.

943. I love you for the hundred cute nicknames you invent on the spot.

944. I love you because you back me up in every crazy idea I might come up with.

945. I love you because you flirt with me every day, for years now.

946. I love you for the stars in your eyes whenever you look at me.

947. I love you for the way you pull my hair and even make me like it.

948. I love you because you catch me if I fall.

949. I love you because you're so sexy when you smoke your long slim cigarette.

950. I love you for how you passionately yell at the TV even if you have no idea who's playing.

951. I love you because I make you shiver whenever I touch you.

952. I love you for the way you raise your right eyebrow when you don't like something.

953. I love you because to this day you have not learned to whistle.

954. I love you because you use sarcasm and irony with such excellence.

955. I love you because you've turned my world upside down.

956. I love you because your eyes make me want to take my clothes off.

957. I love you because you know and accept all my flaws.

958. I love you because when something goes wrong I know who to call for a kind word.

959. I love you because you accept all my friends just because you know they are part of my life.

960. I love you because you know how to shut up when you feel like saying much.

961. I love you because you showed me beauty where I did not think beauty can exist.

962. I love you because you taught me that the first person to love me should be myself.

963. I love you because should I die tomorrow I would have known what love really is.

964. I love you because when I dream of my old days, the only person with whom I see myself is you.

965. I love you because I thank God every day for bringing you into my life.

966. I love you because you encourage and believe in me.

967. I love you because you let me go.

968. I love you because you make me come so strong.

969. I love you for you take care of me.

970. I love you for your honesty.

971. I love you because the entire universe conspired to help me find you.

972. I love you because you give me strength to be me.

973. I love you because you know how to make me laugh with tears.

974. I love you because you show me that you love me not just for Valentine's Day.

975. I love you because your kindness is a higher form of beauty.

976. I love you for your moments of madness.

977. I love you because all my orgasms depend on you.

978. I love you because we can talk with our eyes.

979. I love you for who I am when I'm with you.

980. I love you because the best memories of my life start with you.

981. I love you because you always make me smile with no reason.

982. I love that you showed me what it means to wake up with a smile on my face.

983. I love you because of the peaceful story your eyes tell me on each stormy night.

984. I love you for your totally crazy moments.

985. I love you for being able to say everything with one look and no words.

986. I love you for who I am when I'm with you.

987. I love you because the best memories of my life start with you.

988. I love you for standing beside me in those moments when I was lacking my mental sanity.

989. I love you for making me the best presents ever.

990. I love you because sometimes you're funny, even if you don't want to.

991.

992.

993.

994.

995.

996.

997.

998.

999.

1000.

www.ingramcontent.com/pod-product-compliance
Lightning Source LLC
Chambersburg PA
CBHW060357050426
42449CB00009B/1772